Gary Vaynerchuk
With 0 F*cks

How GaryVee is Inspiring Millions of People

IVAN FERNANDEZ

Text Copyright © Ivan Fernandez

Legal & Disclaimer

The information contained in this book is not designed to replace or take the place of any form of medicine or professional medical advice. The information in this book has been provided for educational and entertainment purposes only.

The information contained in this book has been compiled from sources deemed reliable, and it is accurate to the best of the Author's knowledge; however, the Author cannot guarantee its accuracy and validity and cannot be held liable for any errors or omissions. Changes are periodically made to this book. You must consult your doctor or get professional medical advice before using any of the suggested remedies, techniques, or information in this book.

Upon using the information contained in this book, you agree to hold harmless the Author from and against any damages, costs, and expenses, including any legal fees potentially resulting from the application of any of the information provided by this guide. This disclaimer applies to any damages or injury caused by the use and application, whether directly or indirectly, of any advice or information presented, whether for breach of contract, tort, negligence, personal injury, criminal intent, or under any other cause of action.

You agree to accept all risks of using the information presented inside this book. You need to consult a professional medical practitioner to ensure you are both able and healthy enough to participate in this program.

Table of Contents

The Book at a Glance

If you are into entrepreneurship, startups, and self-help, you may have already heard of Gary Vaynerchuk; but how much do you really know of him? Is he for real or is he just another glorified snake oil merchant?

Gary Vaynerchuk is a serial entrepreneur, best-selling author, investor, and inspirational speaker. He owns one of the most popular digital marketing company in New York called Vayner Media.

He has four best-selling books – "Crush It!", "The Thank You Economy" , "Jab, Jab, Jab, Right-Hook", and "#AskGaryVee: One Entrepreneur's Take on Leadership, Social Media, and Self-Awareness."

Gary Vaynerchuk (or Gary Vee) is not famous at all, at least in mainstream media, but he is internet-famous. He rose to prominence as the "internet wine guy." He is also a self-proclaimed social media master and branding expert. He documents his business exploits almost daily on YouTube. This is the reason why many people roll their eyes when they hear his name. The New York Times and the Wall Street Journal called him a notorious self-promoter and an overexposed entrepreneur.

Nevertheless, Gary Vaynerchuk is a classic example of someone fighting for and living the American dream. He came from a poor, Russian immigrant family. His parents barely spoke any English when they arrived in the United States.

This is the story of Gary Vee's journey from rags to riches, a story of how passion, will, and plenty guts can help you reach an impossible dream. This book is written based on hundreds of articles, books, stories, videos, and interviews that Gary Vee either made appearances or written.

Gary Vaynerchuk is real. He is as real as the American dream. Everyone knows a little bit of Gary's story. However, you are about to discover his entire story – his childhood, his dreams, his business strategies, and why he has become an inspiration.

Introduction

Gary Vaynerchuk is loud and unapologetic. He uses crude language when he talks to his audience, and he also has heightened self-awareness and self-confidence; he knows who he is and who he is not. Love him or hate him; Gary Vee is the next big thing in the digital marketing and branding industry, and he is just getting started.

Nevertheless, where did Gary Vaynerchuk come from? How did he become an overnight sensation? Well, he is hardly an overnight sensation. Not even close. Gary Vee spent years hustling and climbing just to get to where he is right now, and he started when he was still a child.

In 1978, Gary's poor Russian-Jewish family came to the United States to seek asylum from the oppressive regime of the USSR. His father worked as a stock boy in a wine shop, and his family lived in a small studio apartment in Queens. Vaynerchuk recalled back when he was young he wanted a New York Jets jersey, but his family could not afford to buy the authentic merchandise, so his mother knitted one for him. This was a turning point in Gary's life because that is when he started dreaming big; he dreamed of owning the New York Jets. Today, Gary is still chasing that dream, but his life today was far from what he had experienced when he was a child. He is now a multi-millionaire working in the digital marketing industry. He has already written four best-selling books and spoke to the most prominent tech and startup conferences.

This book tells a riveting story of a man who believed in himself so much that he got the Fortune 500 companies to believe in him too. This is a story of hope, passion, and persistence. A story of how Gary transitioned from running a small lemonade franchise, transitioning to a vast wine e-commerce shop, to currently being a digital marketing guru.

This is a story of passion, hope, and persistent pursuit of wealth and success.

[IMPORTANT]

Exclusive Premium Bonuses

As a way of saying thanks for downloading this book, we'd like to offer you our premium bonuses (value: $7.98)

What will you receive?

1) A premium 3 page pdf summary of this entire book (value: $3.99)

2) An exclusive printable pdf of Steve Jobs top quotes – you can print it out and paste it on the walls in your office or in your house! (value: $3.99)

Claim your bonuses easily by clicking <u>here</u> or scrolling to the last page of this book!

P.S. Please do not share what you're about to receive. Strictly no resale of the bonuses is allowed. Click <u>here</u> or scroll to the last page of this book now to claim your free bonuses.

Chapter 1: Who is Gary Vee?: Gary Vaynerchuk's Life In A Nutshell

Before we take a trip down memory lane, we will discuss who Gary Vaynerchuk is. What does he do, and why does his story matter?

Gary Vaynerchuk is your typical New Yorker – driven, loud, strong-willed, and always in a rush. You have probably seen him virtually everywhere. In fact, he is one of the few entrepreneurs who have a solid fan base, which he fondly calls "Vayniacs." What's fascinating about Gary is not just his business acumen, but his passion and authenticity. He says just about anything he wants to say and does not use a filter.

Gary Vee, as he is fondly called by his clients and employees, has already established himself in the business world. He was in Crain's and Fortune's 40 Under 40. He was featured in huge publications such as Time, GQ, The Los Angeles Times, The New York Times, NYMag, Entrepreneur, and The Wall Street Journal. He has appeared on many television appearances on Bloomberg TV and CNBC; in mainstream talk shows such as Ellen DeGeneres Show (September 2007), Late Night with Conan O'Brien (August 2007 and May 2008),

Nightline (October 2007), The Big Idea with Donny Deutsch (May 2008), Mad Money with Jim Cramer (May 2008), Late Night with Seth Meyers (2014), On the Money (2015), and The View (2017 with Will.i.am and Jessica Alba). In 2008, he also attended an Authors@Google web video. He has a YouTube channel called the Wine Library TV that started in 2006 when the platform was only four months old. The channel has more than a thousand episodes, but Gary decided to stop publishing new videos in 2012 to focus on his digital marketing entrepreneurial project. However, in 2014, Gary started another YouTube channel called "Ask Gary Vee" where he answers questions from his followers. He also established another web series called DailyVee, which chronicles his daily exploits as an entrepreneur in the greatest city in the world – New York City. Thus, when The Wall Street Journal called him an overexposed entrepreneur, they are partly right.

Gary Vaynerchuk is an entrepreneur, venture capitalist, a social media star, author, and keynote speaker, but before he became all that, he started working in his family wine business Shopper's Discount Liquor, he was 14 at the time. He learned about the internet in 1994 when he was a college freshman at Mount Ida College, and right away, he knew it was special. He discovered the beauty and wonders of e-commerce in 1996. Therefore, that year, he convinced his dad to hire a full web developer. The following year, he launched one of the first wine e-commerce sites in the United States – www.winelibrary.com. When he graduated in 1998, he started running the wine shop and entirely concentrated on the shop's website in 1999. He used e-mail marketing, banner advertising, and e-commerce to increase the revenue of his father's business from $3 million a year to $60 million, and he did this within five years.

In 2006, he started a show called Wine Library TV on YouTube. That show gained a cult following among wine connoisseurs and already has more than 1,000 episodes before Gary stopped making more videos. The channel is still around, but the last episode was from 2016. His time in Wine Library TV made Gary realized that he has a knack for speaking and inspiring people. Shortly after, he became famous and started guesting in different TV shows.

In 2009, Gary decided to establish a digital marketing company with his brother, AJ, called Vayner Media. He started writing books about entrepreneurship and following your passion. He wrote four best-selling books, namely "Crush It!", "Jab, Jab, Jab, Right Hook", "The Thank You

Economy", and "#AskGaryVee: One Entrepreneur's Take on Leadership, Social Media, and Self-Awareness."

Today, he has two web shows the DailyVee and the #AskGaryVee Show where he had interviewed some famous guests such as Tony Robbins, Jewel, Arianna Huffington, and John Legend. He currently stars in "The Planet of the Apps" with Gwyneth Paltrow, Will.i.am, and Jessica Alba; this is the first reality show produced by Apple.

He established two more companies – a publishing company called VaynerX and an athlete representation agency called VaynerSports. He invested in more than 50 profitable internet ventures, including Facebook, Snapchat, Uber, Venmo, and Twitter. He currently also runs VaynerRSE – a $25 million investment fund that focuses on creating startup incubators and investing in technology and various passion projects. As of writing, he is worth about $150,000,000.

As of writing, Gary is 42 years old. He is at the peak of his health and his career as an entrepreneur and social media star. He is still hustling, waking up at 6 am every day, and working until the wee hours of the morning. He hosts web shows and continues to help large companies improve their digital presence.

What sets Gary apart from all the other entrepreneurs is that he is always thinking ahead. He had used e-mail marketing before it was a thing. He was even one of the e-commerce pioneers in the wine and liquor industry. Gary keeps moving forward. He keeps on thinking of ways to be one step ahead of his competitors.

Gary has come a long way from being a poor Russian immigrant child to being a multi-million American entrepreneur. He has yet to fulfill his dream of buying the New York Jets, but he is not in a rush. He knew that eventually, it is going to happen. He is just getting started.

In the next chapters of this book, we will take a look back to one of the most amazing stories about guts, perseverance, self-confidence, and self-belief. Believe it; this is not a story about luck. It is a story about hard work, passion, talent, and a lot of heart.

Chapter 2: Coming to America: The Early Years of Gary Vaynerchuk

Many people thought that Gary Vaynerchuk came out of nowhere and became a millionaire overnight. That is hardly the case. Gary was not an overnight sensation. He actually came from the humblest of roots; he came from an immigrant family who escaped Soviet Russia.

Gary was born in a city called Babruysk in Belarus (now known as Byelorussia). He was born in a Russian Jewish family. His father, Sasha, is in the construction business while his mother Tamara is a homemaker. They were married in their early 20s. Both of his parents grew up in the Soviet Union. The Soviet Union, at that time, was a dark, unhappy, and scary place, especially for Jews. The government produced low-quality goods, and their supply was often low. There were shortages of the essential products like medicines, clothes, meat, toilet paper, and personal hygiene goods. Luxury wares such as fashionable clothes, high-quality make-up items, stylish blue jeans, American cigarettes, and even toilet paper were only available to high-ranking government officials.

People in Belarus were so poor that it was normal for two to three families sharing a small studio apartment. This situation leads to stress, disagreements, overcrowding, and feuds. The government discouraged its citizens from owning cars. Only a few high-ranking Communist Party members have access to expensive cars. It was indeed a dark time.

Many of Sasha and Tamara's family members were killed by the government just because they were Jewish. The horrors that the couple faced were unimaginable. Their life was full of heartbreak, disappointments, and pain.

In the early 1970s, Sasha's granduncle moved to the United States. Sasha then discovered how different the life in America was from his days in Belarus. He learned that everyone in America had the opportunity to succeed through hard work and perseverance. He was fascinated by the great American dream. On November 14, 1975, Sasha and Tamara's first child, Gennady, was born. Sasha wanted a better life for his son, so he sought political asylum in the United States. In 1978, Sasha, along with his wife Tamara, his son Gennady, his parents, and grandparents, migrated to the United States. He gave Gennady a new American name, Gary, in the hopes that he would grow up to be a great American man.

Not long after they migrated, Gary's little sister, Elizabeth, was born. All eight members of the Vaynerchuk family crammed themselves into a small studio apartment in Queens, New York. They were so poor that they often did not have enough food.

Sasha got a job as a stock boy in a liquor shop in Clark, New Jersey, and he would commute to and from work every day. When Sasha was established in the liquor shop, the family eventually moved to Dover, New Jersey so that he would be closer to his work. After a while, they moved to Edison, New Jersey, where Gary grew up. Sasha does not speak that much English at that time, but he worked hard. He worked fifteen hours a day so that he could give his family the life he always dreamed. He has a genuine heart of an immigrant. After a few years, Sasha was promoted to an assistant manager, and then, he became the manager of the liquor shop. He continued to work hard and barely had time for his kids. His wife, Tamara, almost single-handedly raised the Vaynerchuk kids.

After years of working, Sasha partnered with a relative of his, and using the money he saved after years of working at the liquor shop; he set up his small liquor store in 1983. He worked harder and could even spend 18 hours in the wine shop.

Gary looked up to his father. He was his hero and inspiration. He saw how hard his father worked for his family. However, he did have a strained relationship with his father while he was growing up, mainly because Sasha was always working. He was in the wine shop most of his waking moment. Therefore, naturally, the Vaynerchuk kids bonded more with Tamara than with Sasha.

Tamara experienced horror and adversity both in Belarus and in the United States. She barely spoke English, and she has to take care of three kids and Sasha's grandparents. Nevertheless, she is a supportive wife and a loving mother. Gary recognized that his success was a byproduct of his mother raised him.

Tamara taught the Vaynerchuk kids the importance of empathy, and taught her kids how to stay grounded and cheered them on when they succeeded at something. She gave them a healthy mix of empowerment, freedom, support, and acknowledgment. She made her kids feel like they could do anything. This gave Gary the confidence to be the best at what he does and chase his dreams.

Boyhood Dream

Gary did not speak English when his family first moved to the United States. He felt left out. One day, when Gary was just five years old, he saw some kids playing football in his neighborhood, and it became his first American "thing." Shortly after he discovered American football, he became a fan of the local New York Jets. Little Gary wanted a six dollar Jets jersey, but his family could not afford one. Therefore, his mom spent two hours a day knitting him a New York Jets jersey.

When he was eight, Gary dreamed of becoming the owner of the New York Jets. He felt like it was his destiny. He wanted to go from a place where his family could not afford a jersey to him actually owning the team. This thought excites and drives him every day until now.

Chapter 3: The Little Mogul: Gary Vaynerchuk's Early Entrepreneurial Exploits

Malcolm Gladwell said in his book "The Outliers" that you need to spend at least ten thousand hours to master a skill, and that is why Vaynerchuk is now a very prolific sales clerk. Gary Vaynerchuk started selling and set up a business at a very young age.

When he was six years old, he would sell lemonade in his neighborhood. He would gather all his friends and get them to sell lemonade in different areas of his surroundings. After a few months, he already owns three lemonade stands. He would ride his bike and collect his cut of the money his other lemonade stands would make for the day; it was as if he was a member of the Russian mob. By the age of eight, he already had eight lemonade stands in his neighborhood.

He has this friend named Eric Conrad, who would only come to Edison, New Jersey, during the summer. Eric was the only friend he had who is good at selling stuff. He always sold more lemonade than his other friends would. Nevertheless, Gary found that Eric has been stealing one or two cups of lemonade every day. However, instead of confronting Eric about this, Gary would just let it go because Eric brought in tons of revenue for his lemonade business. That is the first business lesson that Gary learned. It was then that he knew that he has a knack for entrepreneurship.

Selling and earning money excited him even when he was just a little boy. Every kid in his neighborhood wanted to play, but Gary just wanted to sell stuff. He would wash cars to earn money or put up a small flea market and sell anything he could get his little hands on. He would always come up with excellent ideas to make money.

When he was 11, his mother took him to the US 1 Flea Market. They went in, and Gary met a baseball card dealer. He wanted to buy a couple of packs, and he intended to sell the cards later, but the dealer said, "You need a price guide, so you know what they are worth." The price guide was three dollars, so Gary hesitated because it was a lot of money for young Gary, but he decided to take the chance. He bought the cards and the price guide. He was excited when he got home, opened the packs, and he was surprised to know how much the cards are worth. Therefore, he went all in. He went back to the store and bought more cards. He collected baseball card for about twenty-four months. He would pay more attention to cards than he did in school.

Gary was good at selling, but he did not do well in school. In fact, he averaged Cs and Ds, and sometimes he would get a couple of Fs. At that time, Gary thought that he was a loser. There was a time in his life when he did not believe that he could amount to anything. He did not believe that he would be successful. The good thing was that Gary had a supportive mother. Tamara knew that he was a hustler. She knew that his son was an entrepreneur, so she downplayed the importance of school and highlighted the importance of selling and earning a buck. His mother inspired him to use his selling skills to make something out of himself.

When he was 13, he told his mom that he wanted to go to card shows in malls in New Jersey so he could sell his cards. At that time, he was earning two to three thousand dollars every weekend! It was not bad for a thirteen-year-old. By the time that he was 14, he had already made thirty thousand dollars from his baseball card business. He was phenomenal. Everything was rocking. He was going to be the biggest baseball card dealer of all time, but his dad put a stopper to this dream of his.

When he was 14, he was getting ready to do the biggest baseball card show in New Jersey. He collected all his cards and made sure he was prepared for the show. However, his dad had other plans; he told him that he would be helping in the liquor store. By this time, Sasha was already the sole owner of a liquor store called "Shopper's Discount Liquors." Gary was upset because that meant he could not sell his baseball cards anymore. They argued for a while. However, due to Sasha was the classic Soviet dad, Gary lost the argument and went to the store to help. Gary could not do anything but cry. He cried for forty minutes when he and his dad were commuting from their home to the store. Nevertheless, about two minutes before they got to the store, he found the strength to compose himself. He said, "Dad, how much you are going to pay me?" Then, his dad said, "Two dollars an hour." Therefore, Gary started crying again. It was terrible because, for the next 18 months of his life, he would spend all his weekends at the store, bagging ice and dusting the shelves. He would spend every single day of his summer and Thanksgiving vacation at his dad's liquor store, all for just a measly two bucks an hour. Gary was not happy with this arrangement. However, working for his dad did teach him the value of hard work.

When he turned sixteen, after months of working in the wine cellar, Gary was already allowed upstairs so he could start selling wine, and this changed his life. He was in the store during summer vacation, and every customer would ask for Caymus Special Select 1990. It was Wine Spectator's wine of the year, so it was very popular. Gary has seen countless customers come into the store asking for the wine, and then leave because his father did not have enough of the wine in stock. This awakened the entrepreneur in him that laid dormant for the past couple of years. He thought that it was not practical to let all these customers go just because they did not have enough stock of a famous wine, so he started taking back-orders.

At the time, the store did not have a back-order system in place, but he was not scared. He took out his notebook and pen and talked to the next customer. As expected, the customer asked for Caymus Special Select 1990. He told the customer, "Sir, the wine is sold out as of the moment, but I can take your back-order. Just give me your name, phone number, and address. May I ask how much you would like?". The customer replied, "Six cases." Gary was shocked and thought that the customer might be an alcoholic. Therefore, he asked the customer, "Are you having a party or something?". The customer said, "No. I'm collecting wines."

That was a big light bulb moment for Gary. At that point, he wanted to help his family. He wanted to feel like he can bring something to his father's business. He knew what he could do, and he felt confident.

From that moment on, he poured every ounce of his soul into becoming the biggest wine expert in the country. He started reading wine magazines. He did not listen to his teachers at school. He sat in a science class reading the Wine Spectator. He did not do well in school because he focused on expanding his father's wine business, but at the time, he did not worry because he already knew that he was going to be big.

Chapter 4: College Years and The Wine Library E-Commerce Site

Unlike the other popular internet entrepreneurs of this modern time, Gary was not the techy type. He only used computers to play NFL video games. He did not own a computer until he was about twenty-two years old.

He went to college when he was 18, and at the time Gary was already earning money, so he was not excited about going to college, but his parents sent him to Mount Ida College anyway. For immigrant families, education is the ticket out of poverty. It is the only key to business and career opportunities. Therefore, even when he did not see the value of college education, he headed to Massachusetts to work on his degree, and he would go home every weekend to New Jersey just to help at his dad's wine store. Unlike most of his friends, he did not go to parties or hooked up with college girls.

During his freshman year in college, he hung out with a couple of computer "geeks", and that's the first time he heard about the internet. Not long after, Gary realized that he could use the internet to sell stuff. He already knew that the internet was going to be big and that it is going to be a great marketing platform. When eBay was still in its infancy, Vaynerchuk was already selling stuff on the platform.

Gary thought that the name of their wine shop was extremely unsexy and unattractive. Hence, he asked his father to re-brand their wine business. Sasha traveled to California and visited many wine libraries. Therefore, the father and son duo decided to change the shop's name from "Shopper's Discount Liquors" to "The Wine Library." Gary convinced his father to hire a full-time web developer to help them build an e-commerce site, which was a bit crazy and impractical at that time, but he was convinced that this could really help the shop expand.

In the latter part of 1996, Gary and Sasha launched www.winelibrary.com – one of the first wine e-commerce sites in the United States and the world. In 1998, he became the Director of Operations of the Wine Library and laid out an aggressive marketing plan that could help the business grow. Gary increased the company revenue from three million dollars a year to sixty million dollars a year in just five years.

Like his father, Gary spent fifteen hours a day working in the wine shop. He would do email marketing, print ads, radio, and banner advertising just to get the word out about his father's wine shop. He sat next to the lead web developer in the office named Eric Casnor. Eric helped Gary with all the tech stuff. He discovered cool new things like Myspace and Friendster, and then he found YouTube.

Gary felt that for the last one hundred fifty years, marketing is about "pushing" something. You are literally shoving your idea or your products down other people's throats. Marketing was a one-way street; entrepreneurs to talk about how great their product is and people would just listen; that is it. There is no direct communication with the audience.

However, when Gary discovered social media, he felt that for the first time in 150 years, marketing is all about the "pull." Customers can now openly respond to ads and all other marketing stuff, and they can choose what ads they want to see. There is a massive cultural shift. This was another light bulb moment for Gary. He decided to use YouTube to build his personal brand and become his own man – away from the shadow of his already successful dad.

Life as the Internet Wine Guy

In 2005, although Gary has achieved a lot as the operations director of Wine Library, he was still unknown in the business world. But, then, something happened that would forever change the internet – three former PayPal employees Steve Chen, Chad Hurley, and Jawed Karim launched a video sharing site in February 2005, and they called it YouTube. Gary was mesmerized by this new website and its potential.

On his 30th birthday (November 18, 2005), Gary felt like his life is not on the right track. Although he is already running a multi-million dollar business, he felt like he is still living in the shadows of his Russian dad. He felt like his behaviors were not aligned with his goals. At that moment, he decided to build his personal brand.

He was acquainted with YouTube, and he saw this as an opportunity to build a personal brand and improve the reach of his father's e-commerce site. He saw the video-sharing site as an opportunity to create a competitive advantage and be one step ahead of other liquor e-commerce websites. Gary felt that the wine industry is too conservative; it is full of disdainful shopkeepers who are unwilling to educate their customers about the pros and cons of different wine types, and egotistic sommeliers who think themselves as better than other people just because they have a deeper understanding of wines. This made the wine industry a bit intimidating to newbies. Gary saw this problem as an opportunity to establish wine as a reachable commodity. Hence, he started the first wine video blog called Wine Library TV on February 21, 2006, when YouTube was still young. Wine Library TV was quite special because it was one of the first video blogs in the world.

In the vlog, Gary talked about the "ins and outs" in the wine industry. It gives the viewers an in-depth look at the Wine Library, the liquor industry, and wine in general. This show allowed Gary to display his encyclopedic knowledge of wines and the wine industry. He educated his viewers about the effects of the sun, wind, and soil on the flavor of wine, and gave wine buying tips, valuable information about different wine types, independent wine growers, and big wine brands.

Gary tried his best to entertain and bring laughter to the wine world. His show was rich in both information and humor, and at the same time, it was a breath of fresh air in the once stuck-up world of wines. Slowly, Wine Library TV gained a cult following. Gary called the viewers of the show – Vayniacs. The show featured a long list of wine entrepreneurs, vineyard owners, winemakers, wine lovers, and wine critics including Daniel Rogov, Nicolas Joly, Tim Hanni, Matt Mullenweg, Philippe Melka, Margo Van Staavern,

Walter Raymond, Charlie Meeker, Molly Meeker, Achaval Meeker, David Forsyth, Tony Coturri, and Daniel Johnnes.

The show was an online success, and it cemented Gary's reputation as a wine expert. People in the wine industry now looked up to him, and he used this opportunity to grow his network and connected with other wine entrepreneurs. Nevertheless, then, he started his own social media marketing business. Because of his growing popularity, he got a ten-book deal from Harper Collins. In 2008, he wrote "101 Wines: Guaranteed to Inspire, Delight, and Bring Thunder to Your World." The book did pretty well, so he started going on a book tour. He wrote two more books – "Crush It!: Why Now Is The Time To Cash In On Your Passion" in 2009 which became his first bestseller. Then, he wrote another bestseller "The Thank You" economy in 2011. Gary was so busy with the book tour, so he did not have much time to do Wine Library TV.

Daily Grape

After building Vaynermedia, Gary had to give up his beloved Wine Library TV to focus on his new business. After filming the 1000th episode, on March 14, 2011, he decided to stop posting new videos on the channel to concentrate his efforts on an app called The Daily Grape. The Daily Grape was much like Wine Library TV, but Gary and his tech team also integrated an e-commerce feature into this app. This means that the app allows the customers to buy the wines that Gary features on the show. Like Wine Library TV, the Daily Grape became quite a hit. Gary branded the Daily Grape as the most passionate wine show on the internet, and it really is. Like the YouTube channel, the app allowed Gary to highlight his encyclopedic knowledge about wine. However, he has to cancel the show after the 89th episode on August 23, 2011, because he has to focus on his other dreams. He wanted to achieve something more significant. He wanted to become bigger and finally, step out of his father's shadow. He felt that he is ready to move on and do other things. There were many different projects that he wanted to do.

Wine Library and Daily Grape have been a huge part of Gary's life. It represented almost fifteen percent of his life, and it jumpstarted his career as a social media and marketing guru. He loves wine, but he is an entrepreneur first. Therefore, with a heavy heart, he finally decided to leave the wine show business. Nevertheless, he filmed the 1001st episode on February 21, 2016, to celebrate Wine Library TV. He also shot the 1002nd episode on August 30, 2016. This goes to show that even if Gary Vaynerchuk has grown into a multi-millionaire, a public speaker, and an investor, he would always be the "internet wine guy."

Family

While he was working in his family business, he met a young woman named Lizzie in 2004. He virtually married Lizzie an hour and a half after their first date because something felt right about how she was wired. He knew that Lizzie was also a big picture thinker. Lizzie was independent, and Gary loved her to bits. They now have two children – Xander Avi Vaynerchuk and Misha Eva Vaynerchuk. Gary always says – family first. Even now that he is worth over $160 million, he still knows that his family is his most important possession.

Chapter 5: Gary Vee's Most Important Work - VaynerMedia

Gary loves wine. He loves talking about it. In fact, he made himself famous by talking about wines on YouTube. However, his most important work is not Wine Library- it is VaynerMedia.

When Gary started doing a wine show on YouTube, the sales of his family liquor business went up significantly. Gary knew that he was good at social media marketing. When he was doing the wine show, he was introduced to the who's who of the tech industry and social media marketing.

In 2009, he knew that the world was going through a vast media revolution. People do not watch TV anymore – they watch Netflix to skip all the commercials. They do not read newspapers anymore. When they drive, people do not even look up to billboards anymore; they are too busy checking their smartphones. Therefore, that is when he decided to join the board of Buddy Media, a company that produced social enterprise software that empowers advertisers and helps businesses connect with their customers. The company offers a social media marketing suite that benefit small businesses.

During his time at Buddy Media, Gary saw the need for a social media consulting and branding company. At that time, his younger brother, AJ, just graduated from college. Therefore, he founded VaynerMedia with his brother AJ in 2009 at the conference room of Buddy Media. For a while, he ran his small advertising business in the conference room of Buddy Media. He started with just five employees.

VaynerMedia is a full-service digital advertising agency. They help both small and big businesses build their brands on the internet. They do modern video production, social media marketing plans, content distribution, and influencer marketing.

There were already many digital marketing companies back in 2009, but VaynerMedia was special because one of the biggest online personalities established it. The firm reverse-engineers solutions to marketing problems and places their clients at the center of their new reality. They think of unique ways to boost their clients' online presence, image, and reputation.

VaynerMedia focuses on four social marketing areas – digital business intelligence, social media marketing tools, digital business transformation, and digital first organization. They create product positioning and digital testing models. They also do consumer research and digital audits.

VaynerMedia is committed to building their client's digital brand. They do marketing strategies and content distribution. They even work with various social media influencers to help their clients get a head start. They also paid media like Google Ads, Pay per Click, etc. They also do apply digital marketing consultancy, helping their clients build, test, and then, launch their social media marketing and organization models to expand their business. Today, the firm has 600 employees all over the world. The company employs over two hundred writers, photographers, editors, designers, videographers, and animators to help clients reach their business objectives. As of this writing, the company already has offices in New York and San Francisco. It is also in the process of building offices in Asia, where there is a vast talent pool.

Gary believes that we live in a world with ADHD; no one has the time to watch a three-minute television commercial or read a 500-word blog post. That is why Gary and his team use their digital gold dust to create amazing and catching social media content for their clients.

VaynerMedia has a long list of clients, including PepsiCo, JP Morgan Chase, Dove, GE, Green Mountain, and a number of NFL and NBA teams. This social media agency was so big that it became the main source of Gary Vaynerchuk's wealth.

Chapter 6: Life As A Best Selling Author, Serial Entrepreneur, and Investor

Even when he was a young boy, Gary has big dreams. He did not want to stay in his father's shadow forever. He always wanted to be a prominent multi-media entrepreneur, a rock star in the business world, and wished to "crush it."

When he was selling wines, Vaynerchuk wanted to become a big part of his father's business. Therefore, he became Wine Library's Director of Operations after graduating from college. When he was running his dad's business, he wanted to establish a name for himself, and so, he launched Wine Library TV. When he was running his online wine show, he tried to use his social media influence to build a digital marketing agency called VaynerMedia. Gary just does not stop growing.

Best-Selling Books

Gary did not do well in school, but he is intelligent and brilliant. He has amazing ideas. His brilliance caught the attention of many publishers who want a piece of his mind. Gary got a ten-book deal from publishing giant Harper

Collins for a considerable amount of money. Hence, he started his career as a best-selling author.

101 Wines: Guaranteed to Inspire, Delight, and Bring Thunder To Your World

This book is more than just a regular wine guide; it is a literary masterpiece. It highlights Gary's encyclopedic knowledge of wine and winemaking. Introduce the readers to exotic wines and unique wine flavor, and Gary talked about wine tasting and valuable tips that you can use in savoring the wine.

Gary wrote the book with great enthusiasm, like a little boy who got into Willy Wonka's chocolate factory. At that time, Gary still ran his father's wine business, so it was more than just a book; it was also a marketing tool, mainly because most of the wines featured in this book are available at www.winelibrary.com.

Crush It!: Why NOW Is The Time To Cash In On Your Passion

"Crush It!" is the best and the biggest book that Gary Vaynerchuk has ever written. It was so big that it increased his popularity in the business and marketing world.

Like Wine 101, "Crush It!" was written using an exciting and enthusiastic voice. You could literally feel Gary's passion coming out of every word.

This book talks about how you can turn your passion into a business. Gary outlines how he achieved success by doing the things that he is passionate. It tells the story of how he spent years building his family business in a small local wine shop into a huge e-commerce business and an industry leader. Gary also talks about how to use the power of the internet to harness your passion.

The book is impressive in many ways. First, it was short and succinct. You can finish reading it in just a few hours. Second, Gary talks about how he got started which is very inspiring. Third, it was innovative. Remember that this book was written in 2009 when digital marketing was still pretty young. The ideas written in this book are more relevant nowadays. Gary Vaynerchuk predicted how social media marketing would become the next best thing in branding and advertising.

Here are a few lessons from the book:

1. You just have to start now.

You do not need a lot of money in building a business. You just need to make an effort. Gary believes that the effort is more important than dollars. He believes that no one would make a million dollars with minimal effort unless they win in a casino or a lottery.

2. You have to build a personal brand.

These days, customers are not just interested in the product; they also care about the owner of the company. Building a personal brand is not expensive nowadays; all you need is a social media account.

3. Social media is more significant than traditional marketing.

During his early days at the Wine Library, he used traditional marketing to market his products – billboard, radio ads, and direct mail. He got 170 orders through the billboard, 240 orders via radio ads, and three hundred orders via direct mail and email marketing. In total, he paid more than $7,000 for all marketing channels.

When he opened a Twitter account and started tweeting, the business got 1,700 orders at no cost in just 48 hours. Amazing, right?

4. Put a lot of effort into creating your content.

There is so much noise in social media nowadays. If you want to catch and keep the attention of your potential customers, you must put effort into creating great content. You must also be authentic. Authenticity is the one trait that allows you to crush it and create a personal breakthrough.

5. Create communities to widen your reach.

To expand your reach, you must create communities. You must have a strong cult following and a steady fan base. Early in his career, Gary has established himself as the wine expert. This gave him access to a community of wine enthusiasts and wine lovers.

"Crush It!" is an entertaining book. However, it is also life-changing. It encourages you to cash in your passion and make money doing something that you love. The book is written with heart and passion. Hence, it is no wonder why it's part of the NY Times Bestselling Booklist.

The Thank You Economy

The "Thank You Economy" is Gary Vee's third book and his second best-seller. It reached #2 on the New York Times Bestselling Booklist. This book was written when Gary was already "crushing it" at VaynerMedia. Therefore, this book is not much about passion, but it is more about digital and social media marketing. This book discusses how both big and small businesses can use social media to expand their business.

Here is a list of the lessons from Gary Vaynerchuk's The Thank You Economy:

1. Business leaders must think, as if they are small shop owners. They must create a one on one connection with their customers and stakeholders.

2. You must make sure that every employee is your company is good at customer service.

3. More often than not, customers buy a product because they associate with someone they know. This is the reason why many companies hire celebrity endorsers. This is the reason why you should establish a personal brand. People would go to buy from you if they knew you. Gary used this strategy

for expanding his family's wine business. To increase the revenue of his wine business, he started a YouTube show and established himself as a wine expert. During his early days of Wine Library TV, he responded to his followers' comments and messages.

4.   The communication world is already changing, and you must use this change to your advantage.

"Crush It!" was written for hungry soon-to-be entrepreneurs who wanted to start a business. The Thank You Economy, on the other hand, was written for established business owners, executives, and managers who want to venture into the brave new world of digital marketing.

Jab, Jab, Jab, Right Hook: How To Tell Your Story In A Noisy Social World

This book is a mashup of the essential elements in Gary Vaynerchuck's earlier books – The Thank You Economy and Crush It!. This book contains many detailed social media marketing strategies and techniques.

According to Gary Vee, most companies focus on "right hook" – They aim at their next advertising campaign and sale.

However, companies should focus on "jabbing" – building deep and lasting relationships with their customers.

In this book, Gary Vee emphasized the importance of creating good social media content in branding and advertising. He said that it took radio more than thirty years to reach fifty million people, and thirteen years for television to get to that number, but it only took Instagram around 1 ½ years to reach that many people.

This book talks about the importance of storytelling because there is no sale without a story. Hence, you have to tell your story and get people to hear your story on social networking sites. Storytelling builds your brand equity.

Here is a list of the valuable lessons from the best-selling book
"Jab, Jab, Jab, Right Hook":

1. You should focus on engaging and triggering an emotional response. Emotions are powerful. Gone are the days when it was enough to create high quality content. You must also create content that invokes emotions.

2. No one has the time to read 500 or 1000 word blogs. No one has the time to watch a 20-minute video. If

you want to catch and keep the attention of your audience, you must create micro-content.

3. You should tell your story. That is the only way that you will invoke emotions.

We live in a world where everyone has the opportunity to tell their story of social media. If you want to grow your business on a massive scale, you must be willing to put yourself out there and tell your story.

#Ask Gary Vee: One Entrepreneur's Take On Leadership, Social Media, and Self-Awareness

This book is Gary's fourth and his third best-seller. It is based on his popular online Q & A show called #askgaryvee. In this book, Gary offers honest and surprising answers to different questions about personal development, social media marketing, relationships, and entrepreneurship.

If you are planning to read something that would motivate you to expand your business, try this book. This book provides more than 300 lessons about entrepreneurship and business. It is a collection of 370 questions and answers compiled from different episodes of #askgaryvee. This book discusses a wide array of topics including Facebook marketing, the value of education in business, wine, sports, dreams, investing, public speaking, Snapchat, finding a business party, working with close friends, and passion.

It also talks about self-awareness and how to use it to conquer the challenges of building a business from scratch.

Gary Vee's previous books were written mainly for entrepreneurs. This book was written for a wider audience – students, stay at home moms, employees, and even the unemployed.

Gary Vaynerchuk also has an upcoming book called "Crushing It!: How Great Entrepreneurs Build Their Business And Influence- And How You Can, Too." Gary will release this book in 2018. It looks like he is going to have another best-seller.

Life As A Serial Entrepreneur

As mentioned earlier, Gary already had multiple businesses. He established a lucrative lemonade and flea market business in their neighborhood when he was just in elementary school, in high school, he already had a profitable baseball card dealing business, and he helped his father grow their family's wine business. Therefore, there is no doubt that Gary Vaynerchuk is a serial entrepreneur.

VaynerSports

He is now the CEO and the co-founder of VaynerMedia. He worked with big-name clients such as Sonic, PepsiCo, Johnson & Johnson, Diageo, Turner, Toyota, AB inBev, JP Morgan Chase, Mondelēz, Syfy, GE, and Unilever. He founded the company in 2009 with his brother AJ. Gary is sports fanatic. In fact, his biggest dream is to own the New York Jets. He was fortunate enough to work with prominent name athletes, NBA teams, and NFL teams in VaynerMedia. In 2016, he co-founded VaynerSports with his brother, AJ.

Gary's brother, AJ Vaynerchuk, oversees the day-to-day operations of the business including, marketing, consulting, and endorsements.

VaynerSports is an athlete representation agency that helps the players deal with issues involving their professional careers. The organization has a long list of clients including, Cornelius Edison, Braxton Miller, Matt Paradis, Derrick Morgan, Jalen Reeves-Maybin, Robert Nkemdiche, Jordan Berry, Isaac Whitney II, Kameron Canaday, Jon Toth, Vernon Adams, Walter Powell, and Ross Scheuerman.

VaynerX

In 2017, Gary Vaynerchuk acquired a women's media company called PureWow for twenty million dollars. PureWow is an online magazine that features recipes, beauty tips, home décor, money, literature, and fashion. It was founded by Ryan Hardwood in 2010 along with big names such as Bob Pittman, Mary Wells Lawrence, Joni Evans, Whoopi Goldberg, Lesley Stahl, and Candice Bergen. This online publishing platform publishes national content and local content for big US cities like Dallas, San Francisco, the Hamptons, New York City, Chicago, and Los Angeles.

This acquisition paved the way for VaynerX – a parent company of his publishing and social media platforms, VaynerMedia and PureWow.

It seems like Gary Vaynerchuk is unstoppable and he is planning to acquire more publishing and online marketing platforms in the future.

Gary Vaynerchuk, The Angel Investor

Gary is wise enough to understand that he does not have the energy to create tens or hundreds of companies. Therefore, to grow his wealth, he invested in various companies including Twitter, Tumblr, Facebook, Birchbox, and Uber.

He eventually established a $25 million holding company called Vayner RSE with various business partners, including his brother AJ Vaynerchuk, Phil Toronto, Matt Higgins, and Kerry Kellogg in 2014. The company specializes in seed investments. This venture capital firm has quite an impressive investment portfolio, including Snap, Medium, CoinBase, Shyp, Berne, and Resy. The company is also incubating startups.

Gary understands and practices the old business and investment principle – do not put all your eggs in one basket.

Chapter 7: Inspiring Students and Entrepreneurs

Gary was gaining popularity in the online and the business world, so he decided to use this popularity to inspire others. He started two new internet shows that would help him to motivate others to achieve the things that he has already accomplished. He also decided to venture into public speaking and spoke at various tech events and business conferences.

The #AskGaryVee Show

Not long after Gary stopped posting on The Wine Library TV, he decided to create an online Q & A show called #askgaryvee. The first episode aired on July 31, 2014. This show allows fans to send questions, which Gary then answers in an honest and surprising manner.

There is no doubt that Wine Library TV established Gary as a wine expert and a social media star. Although #askgaryvee helped him develop himself as a business expert, it allowed him to share his two cents to his audience. Each episode has thousands of views and inspired many people to start their entrepreneurial journey.

The show is broadcast live on Instagram and Facebook, and had notable guests, including Jewel, Arianna Huffington, Tony Robbins, John Legend, Lewis Howes, Logic, Jon Taffer, Ryan Holiday, Simon Sinek, Chase Jarvis, Jake Paul, and Casey Neistat.

This show has helped hundreds, if not thousands, of aspiring entrepreneurs, learn new marketing techniques, and grow their business.

The Daily Vee

In his book, "Jab, Jab, Jab, Right Hook", Gary discussed the importance of telling your story on social media. Therefore, in December 2015, Gary decided to practice what he preached and started a YouTube show called The Daily Vee.

This show chronicles his day-to-day life as an entrepreneur, like running companies, traveling to different companies to give keynote speeches, and going to charity galas. He also used this show to communicate messages to his audience, and share his thoughts and inspire other people.

Gary Vee is a great storyteller, and The Daily Vee definitely tells a great story. A story of his triumphs, defeats, challenges, how he works hard behind the scenes, and how he is walking the talk. The Daily Vee is an inspiring show for aspiring entrepreneurs. It is also raw; there is no set or stage. He does this show while walking in the busy streets of New York City or the car. He even records this while he was having dinner with his friends and apprentices. It allows him to share his thoughts about how successful people think or his opinions about Donald Trump. The Daily Vee is Gary's biggest YouTube show. Each episode gets at least one hundred thousand views (on an average).

Gary brings a different kind of energy to his audience. He is honest, raw, and real. He does not filter out what he says. He curses and uses crude language just to get the message across. He delivers powerful and emotional messages that appeal not only in your mind but also to your heart. If you are, feeling like your life is going nowhere or feeling already defeated. Open your browser, go to YouTube, and watch this show.

Life As A Public Speaker

When he was still a struggling entrepreneur, Gary would watch Steve Jobs keynote speeches that he would deliver when launching a new Apple product. Back then, Gary was not interested in iPhones or iPads. He was more interested in how Steve delivered his keynote speech. He was more interested in his story and delivery. This also inspired Gary to establish a career as a keynote speaker.

When his internet shows were starting to gain followers, he was getting speaking invitations from various organizations. These calls increases when he published his first best-selling book, Crush It!.

Gary Vaynerchuk delivered a speech at the prestigious Inc 500 Seminar in 2011, and another keynote speech at Tech Week in Chattanooga, Tennessee. He also spoke at different conferences and seminars in Ontario, Belgium, Portland, Idaho, San Diego, London, and in Icon 2016.

Gary is authentic, and that authenticity helped him to create a deep connection with his audience. Gary has this powerful energy and passion. You can feel this passion and energy whenever he opens his mouth. He is not afraid to tell it as he sees it. His honesty is both inspiring and refreshing. His words awaken every cell in your body and inspire you to take action.

Gary has a strong charisma and a great sense of humor. His speeches are active, on point, and exciting.

Chapter 8: Planet of the Apps and Gary Vee Sneakers

In 2017, Apple launched its first original series, a show about apps that you can watch on Apple iTunes. On the show, startup entrepreneurs pitch their products to the judges, who will then select the apps that will go to the next round. The entrepreneurs who successfully pass the first round get to pitch to the Venture Capitalists so they can sell their apps on the Apple Store. It is like Shark Tank, but just for iOS apps. Zane Lowe hosted the show, and it stars Gwyneth Paltrow, Jessica Alba, Will.i.am, and Gary Vaynerchuk. The show premiered on June 5, 2017.

Although Gary has already gained massive Twitter and YouTube following, the Planet of the Apps gave him genuine celebrity status. Gary was no longer the "internet wine guy", he is now a legit superstar millionaire that inspires millions of people and spend his days with other A-list celebrities.

What's Next For Gary Vaynerchuk?

Gary has achieved many things in life. Today, he keeps himself busy through speaking engagements and acquiring other media companies. However, Gary still believes that he will own the New York Jets one day.

Chapter 9: Gary's Business Principles: Lessons from A Self-Proclaimed Hustler

Gary Vee became the ultimate poster boy of the great American Dream. He became an inspiration to many. Nevertheless, how did he become a successful entrepreneur? What are the secrets of his success?

Here is the list of Gary's top business principles:

1. In business, speed trumps almost everything.

Gary is not the most talented in the world, nor is the most intelligent, but what sets Gary apart from others is that he is quick to take action. He believes that execution is king. He knows that ideas are worthless without implementation.

The business world is highly competitive, and other businesspeople could simply steal your idea if you do not act fast. Speed is everything in business. Gary believes that speed will trump anything and it is more than one billion times more important than perfection.

Therefore, instead of spending a lot of time over-analyzing and worrying, spend your precious time executing. Life is a race and speed is the powerful determinant of business success. You have to implement and execute your ideas as fast as you could. You have emailed your customers back as fast as you could. Hence, do not over think or over analyze. Stop caring about what other people think or do.

Speed is the only thing that matters. If you keep thinking about other people's opinions, you cannot accomplish anything. Let go of your ego because it slows you down. Stop procrastinating. Stop waiting for everything to be perfect. Just do it.

2. Place your bet on your strengths.

Gary was not good in school, and he did not really try to fix that. Instead of focusing on the things that he is not good at, he focused on his strengths. He used his entrepreneurial and marketing skills to keep moving forward and get closer to his dreams. He knew that he is not smart enough to be a scientist or a mathematician, but he is sure that he is smart enough to be a millionaire entrepreneur.

3. Cash in your passion.

Life is short. Hence, do not spend it doing work that you do not like. We live in an exciting time where anyone can make a living out of his or her passion. Take advantage of this. Turn your passion into profit.

If you like sewing clothes, why not start a fashion business? If you love to shop, why not become a fashion buyer or a stylist? That way, you can shop all day without burning a hole in your pocket.

Let's say that you're a Wall Street broker earning $300,000 a year. You are earning good money, but you are unhappy with your job. You spend most of your salary on luxury goods, travel, expensive gadgets, and fast cars just to make you feel better about yourself. You go to fancy clubs and restaurants just to shake off all the work-related stress. Therefore, even if you are earning good money, you are still in debt.

You decided to quit your job and follow your passion for writing finally. You chose to take a writing job with a salary of $110,000 a year. That is significantly lower than what you are usually used to, but because you love your job, you do not feel the need to go to expensive restaurants and buy expensive things to distract you from your unhappy work life. Hence, even if your salary is lower, you will see that you are now in a better financial position that you were when you were working on Wall Street.

4.   Execute your ideas and execute them well.

As mentioned earlier, ideas do not have value if they are not executed well. Days before Uber was born, there was an App called Taxi Magic, which was established in 2008 by a startup called RideChange. This app allowed people book taxis without talking to operators. This app was used in more than twenty-five cities in the United States, including Los Angeles, Washington DC, New York, and San Francisco. The startup had a potential of growing into a multi-billion dollar company such as Uber is today. There were about thirty thousand downloads per day. However, the app had many flaws. First, the company has an arrangement with a travel software company called Concur. This limited the app's reach. It also prevented the startup from attracting investors. Second, it has a long and complicated payment system, which caused a lot of confusion. They have a flawed booking system as well.

Technically, Uber was an idea derived from Taxi Magic. Nevertheless, because it was executed almost flawlessly, it grew and became the multi-billion transportation company that it is today.

The same thing happened with early social media sites like Friendster, Multiply, and Myspace. These sites were fantastic. Moreover, although Mark Zuckerberg will never admit it, these sites influenced the creation of Facebook in some ways. However, Facebook stood out because of its incredible features. It integrated other apps and games.

When it started, Facebook was a David amidst the Goliaths – Myspace and Friendster, but it was built on what other people already created. What is fantastic about Facebook is that it appeals to human curiosity. It allows people to share their thoughts and photos, and they can check out those of other people. This is the reason why Facebook had a more significant engagement rate than its predecessors. It went viral, and it capitalized on the constant rise of smartphones.

Gary Vaynerchuk believes that ideas do not have value unless they are executed, and they are executed well. Do not wait for perfection. Do not wait until you have enough money. Do not wait until you have enough skills. When an idea comes up, do your best to execute it right away. Remember that an entrepreneur is a person who jumps off the plane and builds a parachute along the way.

5. Stop storytelling like it's 2005.

The internet was still young in the early 2000s, and people were so fascinated with it that they would take anything it offers. This was the time when blogging was popular. This was the time when people spent twenty to thirty minutes per day to read what other people had to say. However, that was in the past. We are now in living in a world where ADD (attention deficit disorder) is more common than cold or a cough. People do not have time to read a 500-word blog; that is the truth. This is the reason why Gary Vee believes that entrepreneur should stop storytelling as if it was 2005 or 2007. This is the reason why Gary is a big fan of micro-stories and Snapchat.

6. Content is King. Context is God.

SEO or search engine optimization was popular in the early days of digital marketing. Nowadays, SEO is still important, but it is not everything. Today, quality content that is predicated on the right context beats strategic placement of keywords. Gary Vaynerchuk always says, "Context is king, but context is God." You have to create something that appeals to your audience. You should think about what your brand offers. Make sure that all your website and social media content is aligned and consistent with your brand.

7. Cultivate Self-Awareness

You cannot beat your competitors if you are not aware of who you are – your strengths, preferences, and weaknesses. Gary Vaynerchuk believes that self-awareness is the most critical attribute an entrepreneur must have. You must learn to accept your flaws and play with your strengths.

What is terrific about Gary Vaynerchuk is that he has an incredible self-awareness. He knows who he is and who he is not. He is not one of those deluded megalomaniac entrepreneurs. He knows that he sucked at many things. However, he does not lie to himself as most people do. Gary knows that he is not perfect, and that is okay.

8. Be authentic.

Most millionaires are prim and proper when being interviewed or speaking in front of hundreds of people, but Gary Vaynerchuk is different. He curses most of the time, he uses crude language in his speeches, and this is the reason why people love him.

Here is how you can become more authentic:

- ✓ Get rid of your filters. Be as raw as you can be.

- ✓ Drop your people-pleasing habits. Avoid doing stuff that you do not like just to please other people.

- ✓ Be open about your mistakes. Be honest about what you can and what you cannot do. Do not oversell yourself.

- ✓ Stop seeking approval.

- ✓ Respect yourself. Take care of yourself. Be yourself, but be the best that you can be.

- ✓ Do not oversell yourself, but do not speak badly about yourself either. Be honest about your mistakes and bad decisions, but do not let them define who you are.

✓ Do not do anything to violate your personal moral code. Make sure that your actions are aligned with your principles and beliefs.

✓ Embrace who you are and celebrate your uniqueness. Appreciate how you are different from others. When Gary Vaynerchuk decided to get into the tech business, he has a different business style than most entrepreneurs in the industry. First, he is not as tech-savvy as Bill Gates, Mark Zuckerberg, or Larry Page; he is more of a marketing guy. He did not try to be like Mike Zuckerberg or Elon Musk; he was true to what he was, so instead of building websites and doing other techy stuff, he hired people to do it for him.

Authenticity allows you to connect with your customers, employees, partners, and investors at a much deeper level. When you are not trying to fit into the mold, you stand out. Authenticity gives you a competitive advantage.

55

9. Give A Fuck About Your Customers.

When Gary was sixteen, he was dusting shelves in his father's wine business when he heard an exchange between a customer and the store clerk. The customer said, "I got a flyer in the mail that says Chardonnay is now $4.99, but I got this bottle earlier for $5.99. Can I get my dollar back?"

The store clerk says, "No, we can't do that. But, if you're going to buy another bottle of chardonnay now, you can get it at $4.99." The customer was upset and said, "You know what, you do not have to worry about it because I'm not coming back to this store."

Gary wondered, "Why not? The customer is certainly worth more than a dollar." He believes in the power of taking care of your customers even early on in life.

In 2001, it snowed hard in New Jersey. Typically, the holiday season is the busiest time at the store. However, because of the heavy snow, the store is only selling one case an hour, which is $45. At that time, he was the lead salesman at the store.

A ninety-year-old lady called and asked Gary to deliver a case of wine. Therefore, he grabbed his car and delivered it. His dad was pissed that he left to deliver a $45 case of wine. However, over the next two to three years, that story became the foundation of how he treated each customer.

Gary believes that too many entrepreneurs are running their business with their mind and not their heart. If you want to succeed in business, you must care about your customers. You should follow up with them about their experiences, and most of all, you should show them kindness.

You should not wait and do nice things to your customers when they are already threatening not buy from your company; you should be kind to them while they are still with you. Moreover, taking care of your customers feels good.

10. Treat social media as a storytelling tool and not a distribution tool.

Many small business owners use social media as a selling tool. They sell stuff on Facebook and Instagram. This is okay, but truth be told, social media does not generate as many sales as e-commerce sites do. Therefore, it is a good idea to use social media as a storytelling tool and not so much of a distribution tool.

You should use it to build your brand and tell your story. To do this:

- ✓ Post behind the scenes videos of how your product was made. This will make your followers feel like they are involved in the production process.

- ✓ Share updates about the milestones of your product and your personal journey as an entrepreneur.

- ✓ Share the lessons that you have learned to your followers.

Many entrepreneurs believe that sex sells. This is the reason why product posters and videos are filled with half-naked models. However, Gary Vaynerchuk thinks that emotion sells more. This is the reason why the "Fearless Girl" commercial of the State Street Global Advisors is so moving. It invokes different kinds of emotions, especially in women.

Make sure to invoke emotions when you are telling your story on social media. Tell stories that will indeed touch your followers' hearts.

11. Working smart is good. But, nothing beats hard work

Many self-help experts think that working smart is much better than working hard, but Gary Vaynerchuk believes that there is no substitute for hard work.

To succeed in life, you have to be smart when making daily business decisions, but you also have to work hard. You have to be willing to work ten to fifteen hours a day if you want to build a multi-million company.

12. Get noticed.

When Gary was still running his father's store, he established Wine Library TV to get more attention for the business. His online show became a powerful marketing tool that increased the revenue of the Wine Library exponentially.

Here is what you can do to get noticed:

- ✓ Make sure that you have a strong social media presence. Engage your audience and post content regularly.

✓ Attend the important events and fairs in your industry. If you are in the cake business, make sure to attend bridal fairs. This allows you to display your work to potential investors and clients.

✓ Give away free stuff. For example, if you are new in the fashion industry, no one is going to buy your stuff. Therefore, you have to give away free bags or clothes to fashion influencers like models and celebrities. This is the easiest way to get noticed in the fashion industry.

✓ Do something that is newsworthy. This will get you noticed and will get you featured in a major publication.

13. Work harder than your employees do.

Many entrepreneurs make the mistake of doing less than their employees do. Delegating is good, but if you delegate too many tasks, you will lose sight of the future of your business.

If you want to be a successful entrepreneur, you have to be the most hardworking person in the office. You must work harder than your employees. You must be the first one to arrive in the office, and yes, you are walking the talk. This inspires them to work hard, too.

14. Do what you preach

As mentioned earlier you have to be an excellent example to your employees. If you are all talk and no action, your employees are not going to respect you. Therefore, you have to practice what you preach. Make sure that you are following your company's policy. Keep your promises and always follow through action items for your team.

If you say that you value your employees, do not go around firing people just to increase your profit margin. If you say that you care about the environment, do not engage in unsustainable business practices.

15. Be a secure leader.

An insecure leader wants validation. He wants to be the best person in the office, and he fires people who threaten and destroy his ego.

A secure leader knows that he is not the smartest person in the room, and he is okay with that. If you want your business to grow, hire people who are smarter than you are. You must learn to trust others and accept that other people can do the task well, too. You must also be willing to collaborate with others. Most of all, you must train your employees to become leaders.

16. Know your target market.

There is no one size fits all in business. You will have to cater to a specific market. Even if you are selling distilled water, you must still consider your target market (the people who live in your area) and the price that they are willing to pay for a bottle of distilled water.

To create an effective marketing strategy, you must know your target market intimately. You must know their preferences, needs, gender, and how old they are.

To do this:

- ✓ Determine what particular needs your service or product fills. Who will use your product or service? If you are doing management consulting, then your target market is a group of struggling entrepreneurs. If you are selling clothes for female kids, then your target customers are moms with female kids who are living in your area.

✓ Narrow your market by gender, age, location, and the income level. You cannot market Louis Vuitton products to teenagers simply because they cannot afford them.

✓ Think about the people who will be interested in the value that your product offers. For example, if you are selling native bags that were made in Mexico, you must target people who love exotic stuff. You may also want to target women who are into the boho fashion.

You cannot please everyone, so you should not waste your precious time trying to please everyone. You must focus on satisfying the people who need or want your product.

17. Trust your intuition.

Many entrepreneurs use their heads when making business decisions and that is okay. You should study your numbers and weigh the pros and cons before making an important business decision, but you can only make the right decision if you listen to your intuition. Whenever you have to make a decision, ask yourself what feels right for you. You cannot make right decisions if you have a "black and white" mindset; you also need to consider the gray areas. Your business will not grow if you are always committed to following the rules. Remember that rules were made to solve past problems, not future problems. Is sticking to the rules worth it? What is your inner voice telling you?

Listen to that little voice within you that tells you that some things are worth the risk. That is the only way that you can keep pushing your business forward.

18. Dream big.

Since he was a child, Gary Vaynerchuk dreamed of owning the New York Jets. This is a big dream for someone who came from a poor Russian immigrant family. Gary held on to that dream. Up to this day, he still dreams of owning that football team. That idea drives him every day. It fuels his passion.

Hence, stop playing small and start dreaming big. Believe that you can achieve everything that you have imagined.

19. Don't wait until the time is right.

Gary built his businesses during challenging times. He took over his father's business a few months after the 9/11 incidents. He established VaynerMedia during the economic crash in 2008. If you wait until the time is right, you are going to wait forever. Be bold and continue to pursue your dreams, even during the most challenging times.

20. EQ is more important than IQ.

Emotions are beautiful. They make you feel human. However, if you want to be a successful entrepreneur, you should learn to control your emotions – especially the negative ones. You should learn to manage your stress, disappointment, and anger. You should avoid lashing out to people, especially your employees and customers. To achieve business success, you must develop a really thick skin.

Here are a few tips that can help you improve your EQ:

- ✓ Let go of your mistakes. Learn from them and then, move on.

✓ Practice self-control. Know when enough is enough.

✓ Do not be afraid to embrace change.

✓ Do not let insults affect your self-esteem. However, you must also learn to accept constructive criticisms.

✓ Empathize with people around you.

✓ Accept that you are not perfect and that is okay.

21. Be the first one to discover the gateway drug.

When a particular product has reached a massive scale, you have to find the "gateway drug" that would lead to the next disruption. For example, in 2008 to 2014, SEO was tremendous. Nevertheless, keywords and Google AdWords cannot do so much. Gary figured out a way to disrupt the then popular SEO marketing strategy by using micro-storytelling strategy.

22. Choose the right social media for your business.

Not all social networking websites are the same. In fact, different social networking sites attract different kinds of people. Therefore, you have to know what type of social media your target market is using. If you are looking to market your services to professionals, it is a good idea to use LinkedIn. If you are selling to people between ages sixteen to twenty-one, you should use SnapChat. If you are selling to people between ages 30 to 55, it is a good idea to use Facebook. If you are targeting people between ages eighteen to twenty-nine, it is a good idea to use Instagram or Twitter.

23. Pay attention to your cash flow.

The reason why people build a business is to make money. You must make sure that your business is making money and that you have a positive cash flow. To do this, you must manage your expenses. You should make sure that you have a reasonable profit margin. Then, create a back-end product that gives you an opportunity to generate higher price points. For example, if you are in the SEO marketing business, you can offer a free consultation to your client and then, shoot up the prices of your other services like keyword research, content optimization, keyword density analysis, press release, media distribution, and pay per click.

24. Do not focus on what your competitor is doing.

Competitive analysis is functional, but focusing too much on what your competitors are doing limits your creativity. Instead of continually checking what your competitors are doing, focus on your customers, on improving your products, and on expanding your business.

25. Get a mentor.

Gary Vaynerchuk's most significant business mentor is his dad. Sasha taught him the value of hard work and honesty. However, if your parents are not entrepreneurs, then you should start looking for a business mentor.

Mentors can give you valuable and practical tips. They can also connect you with a few people who can potentially help grow your business – investors, partners, suppliers, and customers. Your mentor can help you improve your self-discipline, strategic thinking, and people skills. He or she can also help you stay grounded and curb your enthusiasm if necessary.

26. Be ready to embrace new marketing tactics.

Gary Vaynerchuk said that people often fall in love with the way they built their business and the way they made money because it is working. However, if you want sustainable business success, you must spend five to twenty percent of your time thinking of innovative marketing tactics. There was a time when e-mail marketing was the Holy Grail of internet marketing. However, with the emergence of social networking sites, email marketing has slowly lost its magic.

27. Do not micro-manage your employees.

Micromanagement leads to low employee morale, attrition, and high employee turnover. It decreases productivity.

Micromanagement affects the home and work life of your employees. It also affects your work and home life.

You spread yourself too thin if you spend most of your time breathing on your employees' neck. To avoid micromanaging, you must hire the best employees, train them well, and then, trust that they will do a good job.

28. PR is B2B, social media marketing is B2C.

Gary Vaynerchuk sees PR as a B2B (business-to-business) strategy and not a B2C (business to customer) strategy. If you are a PR person, you are helping your client get press in the New York Post, ESPN, The Wall Street Journal, Daily News, Newsday, and the New York Post. You are dealing with gatekeepers. Nevertheless, when you are doing social media marketing, you are directly dealing with your customers and fans. It is more like B2C (business to customer).

29. Build a personal brand.

If you want to build a multi-billion business, you must establish yourself as a personal brand so you would have a competitive advantage. For example, VaynerMedia became one of the most popular digital marketing agencies in New York and the United States simply because of Gary Vaynerchuk's popularity and reputation. If you want to be a Goliath in your industry, you must establish yourself as an expert.

When Gary was still in the wine business, he established Wine Library TV to display his knowledge of wine and liquors. Not long after, he was dubbed as the "internet wine guy" – that became his personal brand. Wine Library's sales went up because of his growing popularity and cult following.

This was when Gary realized that he is good in digital marketing. Therefore, he started his website www.garyvaynerchuk.com. He wrote blogs. He also started talking to students and aspiring entrepreneurs, and launched two new shows "DailyVee" and "#AskGaryVee." He also wrote four best-selling books. These shows and books helped Gary position himself as a social media guru, motivational speaker, and an expert entrepreneur. This is the reason why big brands like PepsiCo chose VaynerMedia as their digital marketing agency.

Here are a few tips that you can use to build your personal brand:

✓ Start building your reputation by writing about the industry in which you are involved. You can start a blog or write a book. You can also create a vlog like what Gary Vaynerchuk did.

✓ Create a social media page and start posting high-quality content- something that makes your followers and fans yearn for more.

✓ Offer to speak in front of a group of students or at an event.

✓ You should invest time in networking. To look like an industry giant, associate yourself with industry giants. This is what Gary Vaynerchuk did. Exposures to people who are more intelligent and successful than you change your perspective and help you adopt a "growth mindset."

✓ Highlight your talents and strengths to your customers and potential investors.

✓ Be your best self, but be yourself. Do not try to be someone else.

✓ Add a short bio to your social media accounts. Make sure that this bio is well written. When you are still starting, you will probably meet your first customers online. So, keep your social media accounts clean and professional. Do not post a photo of a wild weekend in Belize.

Building a personal brand helps you stand out. It enables you be one step ahead of your competitors.

30. Hire an assistant.

You would have to do everything by yourself when you are starting. When Gary was still working at his father's wine business, he handled all the marketing work all by himself. Nevertheless, if your company were already growing, it would be wise to get an assistant. An assistant can take repetitive and straightforward tasks off your plate so you can focus on tasks that are more important.

31. Word of mouth is still the most powerful marketing technique.

Gary Vaynerchuk said that there are two ways to empower your social media community to purchase your product and recommend it to their family and friends:

- ✓ You must create a good product. Make sure that it is worth every penny.

- ✓ Be honest with your customers as to what you want from them. Encourage them to spread the word about your product.

Exaggerating your product features can backfire. Be honest, as much as possible, about what your product can and cannot do.

32. Get good teammates.

You cannot do it alone. Gary Vee has built a personal brand, but he usually works with partners. When he was just starting, he was a part of the "father and son" team behind the wine library. He established VaynerMedia with his brother AJ.

Remember that two (or more) heads are better than one. Therefore, consider getting a business partner.

Here is a list of things that you should look for in potential business partners and team members:

- ✓ Get a business partner that complements you. If you are overly optimistic, get a partner that is pragmatic.

- ✓ Pick someone that you trust.

- ✓ Make sure that your business partner is just as committed as you are. Do not pick someone who is going through a major life-changing event.

- ✓ Pick someone who is willing to work with a team – a team player.

- ✓ Choose someone who is reliable. Someone who keeps his words.

Complainers are like a plague. Avoid collaborating with someone who complains a lot. Choose positive and competent people who have excellent people skills, high EQ, and great personality.

33. Hiring someone is an emotional decision, not a financial decision.

Many experts believe that hiring someone is a financial decision, but Gary Vaynerchuk believes that hiring someone is more of an emotional decision. You do not have to hire the best, but you do need to hire a person whom you could harmoniously work with. Hire someone who is passionate and trustworthy. You should listen to your heart and your gut. Throw away your checklist. Listen to what your gut is telling you. People can write anything on their resumes, so just trust your intuition. Do you think that this person is fit for the job? Do you feel that the candidate can get along well with your team? Do you think that the candidate is passionate about your business?

34. Do things for free.

If you do not have enough money for marketing, you will be willing to do things for free just to gain exposure. If you are a photographer, do pro-bono work for small magazines and websites. If you are in the cake business, you may have to give away free cakes to food bloggers and food critics.

35. You should use the right combination of enthusiasm and action.

Enthusiasm is good because it motivates you and your employees. Enthusiasm is infectious, but that alone will not get you far in business. You have to balance it with action.

36. Provide value up front.

If you want to get your customers' attention and keep it, you have to provide value up front. Here is how you can do this:

- ✓ Create a high-quality product. Make sure that what you are selling is worth every penny. If you own a restaurant, you must sell good food. Good marketing can only do so much.

- ✓ Focus on customer satisfaction. Always think about what your customer wants or needs. Also, take time to ask your customers for feedback. That is the only way that you will know if you are meeting their needs or not.

✓ Giving away free products is the best way to provide value up front. For example, if you are selling tickets for a motivation workshop/speaking engagement, you may want to give away a short e-book to potential buyers.

✓ Let your customers feel that you understand them.

Starbucks does not serve the best coffee in the world, but they do have some of the best customer service. They also have clean, attractive, and cozy shops, so they are providing upfront value to their customers.

37. Reply to every message and comment.

You must act like a small shop owner no matter how big your business is. You must take time to reply to every message and comment of your customers. If you do not have the time to do this, then hire someone to do this for you. You can also set auto-replies, so you do not have to check your Facebook page every minute or every hour.

When you reply to a message or a comment, you are telling your customers (or potential customers) that their concerns are significant. This makes them feel important.

38. Be aggressive in acquiring your first ten customers.

Acquiring your first ten customers is the hardest. So, during the early few days of your business, adopt an aggressive marketing strategy and ask everyone you know to buy your product. Your first ten customers are usually your friends and family. Also, advertise your products in niche forums. For example, if you are selling car accessories, post a link to your e-commerce website for car and racing forums.

39. Do not waste your time chasing unicorns.

Getting a billion dollar valuation like Dropbox, Uber, Grab, Credit Karma, Lazada, SurveyMonkey, Reddit, Quora, Facebook, Alibaba, and Twitter is fantastic. However, these businesses were called Unicorns for a reason; they rarely exist. If you want to make it in the world of business, you must stop trying to be a unicorn and slowly build your company from the ground up. You have to be patient. Do not lose heart if you did not get a billion dollar valuation during your first year.

40. Dump your loser friends.

This may sound harsh, but if you want to increase your success potential, you must surround yourself with people who are more successful than you are. Remember that you are the average of the five people that you spend most of your time. Hence, avoid lazy and cynical people. They will only drag you down and keep you from achieving the life that you have always dreamed for yourself and your family.

41. Be honest and be true to your principles.

When Gary first officially joined his father's company as the lead salesman, he would say just about anything to sell a bottle of wine. His father noticed this and called him out. His father said, "Gary, if you want to stay long in this business, you must practice integrity."

Gary was a talented sales clerk when he was in his early 20s, but he was full of crap. When he started to adopt a more honest approach to selling, that is when the sales of the wine shop skyrocketed.

If you want your business to last for a very long time, you have to be honest with your customers. You must be a principled businessperson. You should draw the line between what you are willing, and what you are not willing to do to make a buck.

42. Small things can make the difference.

You do not have to do big things all the time to succeed in business. Sometimes, the little things count. So, reach out to a customer. Answer a complaint. Listen to your employees. Be on time. Keep your promises. These little things can do so much for you and your business.

43. Give credit where credit is due.

Gary Vaynerchuk sometimes makes it appear as if he did it all by himself, but if you study his life and watch his videos closely, Gary is actually very appreciative of the people around him. He always gives credit where credit is due.

He always believed that he would not be successful if not for his parents. He knows that his success is just a byproduct of how his parents raised him. Gary once said, "Whenever I say that I am the best, what I really meant was that my parents are the best."

He also gives credit to the people he worked with, especially his CTO, Eric. He believed that he would not thrive in the internet business if not for Eric and his team.

When you achieve great success, it is tempting to hoard all the credit. Nevertheless, giving credit where credit is dues does not only make you more likable. It also keeps you grounded. It keeps you real.

44. Adopt the right attitude.

You cannot succeed in life in you do not have the right attitude. As mentioned earlier, entrepreneurship is not an easy path to take. It is full of hardships and heartaches. If you are a pessimist, you are just going to give up easily. Therefore, it is essential that you develop the habit of looking at the bright side of things. Things may not look good now, so what? It is going to get better. Instead of wasting time on your problems, focus on your solution. Focus on how you can develop yourself and become the best that you can be.

45. Be the first one to use a new technology or platform.

Do you know who Michelle Phan is? Well, in case you do not, Michelle Phan is a makeup artist who has an online makeup tutorial channel on YouTube. She was the first real YouTube superstar, but she is not the best make-up artist in the whole world. If you type in the keyword "makeup tutorial" on YouTube, you will find more makeup artists who are better than her.

However, Michelle Phan was the first makeup artist who used YouTube as a platform to display her skills. Because she took advantage of the platform, Michelle Phan is now making millions of dollars out of her YouTube tutorial videos. She became the darling of the makeup and beauty industry. She won multi-million endorsement deals, and she eventually established her own company.

The same thing happened to Gary Vaynerchuk. Gary always made sure that he is one of the pioneers that use a specific technology. When the internet came out, and eBay was created, he was one of the very first eBay sellers. He was also one of the first ones to establish a wine e-commerce site. He was also an e-mail marketing pioneer, taking advantage of it as early as the late 1990s.

When Gary heard about SEO and digital marketing in the early 2000s, he took advantage of it quickly. He created the first wine vlog on YouTube, and he was one of the pioneers of social media marketing.

You see, you do not have to be the best to succeed in business, but you have to be one of the first in the industry. You have to be a pioneer. That is the only way that you can gain a momentum and be one step ahead of your competitors.

46. Do not be afraid of failure.

Fear of failure is crippling. It keeps you from getting what you want. It prevents you from taking action.

According to Gary Vaynerchuk, everyone is afraid to fail, especially in front of his parents. Coming from an immigrant family, Gary was afraid to fail for a while. He was afraid of disappointing his parents. However, you cannot allow your fear of failure cripple you forever. At some point in your life, you have to accept that you are going to fail at some point in your life and that is fine.

47. Never underestimate the value of a comment.

Gary shared in one of his keynote speeches how replying to a comment led to a seventy thousand dollar business transaction. You must never underestimate the value of replying to a comment. You have to pay attention to your followers, and what they have to say about it.

48. No matter what product you produce, your company will always be a media company first.

It is important to make a high-quality product, but sometimes it is not enough. You have to spread the word about your company, and what it offers. Regardless of what you do or whatever it is that you produce, your business will always be a media company first.

Use this knowledge to get ahead. If you do not have a Facebook page for your business, create one. You cannot sell your products if no one knows about it. Start using social media not only to promote and sell your product but also to tell your story.

49. Your actions are being spread around.

Whatever you do, good or bad, is being spread around at this very moment. Therefore, you have to pay close attention to how you are treating your customers. If you are treating them like crap, many people are going to hear about it.

When Gary was helping in his father's wine business, an old woman called complaining that the wine that she ordered got lost in the mail. The carrier must have mixed it up. She was very upset because she has a party coming up and it was the holiday season. Therefore, Gary left the store during peak hours and drove to the old woman's house to deliver a case of wine. That did not make a lot of difference. However, it did to Gary. At that moment, he was committed to giving the best customer service that one can offer. Pay attention to the complaints of your customers and never underestimate their value. Because one unsatisfied customer can cost you hundreds, if not thousands of potential customers.

50. Invest in human connection

We live in a time that is ruled by technology and apps. More and more people are alienated from each other. If you want something meaningful and something that would actually last, you have to establish human connection. You must invest in hiring great customer service staff. You must go an extra mile to make your customers feel valued.

Building your own business is not an easy thing to do. You have to be brave. You have to be resilient. You must care about other people, and you must be willing to put yourself out there. That is what Gary Vaynerchuk did and if it worked for him. It can work for you, too.

Chapter 10: Gary Vaynerchuk's Life Lessons

Gary Vaynerchuk is not just an entrepreneur. He is also a guru. He continues to inspire many people. He spends his days motivating other people to be successful at whatever they choose to do in life.

1. Do not waste your life doing something you hate.

Life is too short. Hence, why waste it doing something that drives you insane? To live a happy life, you must spend it doing what you love. You must do what you are passionate. If it is not fun, do not do it.

Gary was born an entrepreneur. It is in his blood. It makes him happy. For a while, he loved selling wines. He loved being the star of the Wine Library TV. He loved talking about wines. Nevertheless, he knew that it was not the perfect business for him. Gary loved wine, but he loves talking more. He likes building brands. He is good at marketing. He felt like he cannot fully utilize all his skills if he stayed in the wine business and he was right.

After working for his father's business for ten years, he left to establish the most important work of his life – VaynerMedia. This activity allows him to do the one thing that he is really good at – selling ideas and motivating people. He stopped making videos for Wine Library TV and started two new YouTube channels - #AskGaryVee and DailyVee. He wrote best-selling books, and he began speaking to students and entrepreneurs. Gary felt that for the first time in his life, he is doing something that really makes his heart leap. For the first time, he stepped out of his father's shadow and established a successful business.

2.   Spend time with people who matter to you.

People do not wish that they had spent more time in the office when they are on their deathbed. Hard work is necessary, but you should not forget the real reason why you are working hard. Do not forget the people who matter to you.

Gary is a hardworking person, and he would work fifteen hours on most days, but he spends his Sundays with people who are important to him. Never lose sight of the things that are important to you. Incorporate family time into your weekly schedule. Take your spouse on dates. Go to your kids' family days at school. Invite your parents over for lunch now and then.

Work hard to build wealth, but do not spend all your time trying doing it. At the end of the day, your real treasure is your family.

3.   You need to balance confidence and humility.

Many people think that Gary Vaynerchuk is a self-promoting jerk, and to a certain degree, it is true. Gary has spent hours upon hours building his brand. He spent hours talking to his followers on SnapChat and YouTube. As of this writing, he appears in two web series, and he has a show with Jessica Alba, Gwyneth Paltrow, and Will.i.am. He is not afraid to promote himself and say that he is good at what he does. However, that is only one side of the coin. Gary has heightened self-awareness. This helps him identify the things that he does not have enough experience to do them. This allows Gary to balance confidence and humility. He knows that he is good at what he does, but he is also aware that there are tons of other things that he cannot do.

Gary seems like he is overconfident nowadays. Nevertheless, if you look at his old videos, you would see a different version of Gary Vaynerchuk. You will see someone who was a bit unsure of himself. You would see someone who thought that he would not amount to anything. This humility and vulnerability made Gary more attractive to his clients, partners, and social media fans.

To succeed in life, you have to maintain a balance between humility and confidence. You must be confident enough to know that you are good, but you must also have a teachable spirit. Do not be too proud to learn new stuff.

4.   Hook up with more chicks when you are 21.

What Gary Vaynerchuk meant when he said "Hook up with more chicks when you are 21" because you are going to be young only once. So, have fun. You still have a lot of time to reach your goals.

When he was 18 to 21, Gary did not spend a lot of time with his friends. He did not attend wild parties. He was too busy helping his family with the wine business. This is one of his biggest regrets. You are only going to be

91

young once so make sure that you make the best out of it.

5. Be a good listener.

Gary was smart, but he sucked at academics. At one point in his life, he thought that he was a loser and he is not as good as anyone else. This part of his life allowed him to listen to what others have to say.

Gary is now a confident multi-millionaire. However, even if he already made it in the business world, he still listens to other people.

6. Practice empathy.

You would hear Gary pumped up and cursing on social media, but Gary is not a jerk like Steve Jobs was. He does not drive his employees crazy just to earn a profit. He empathizes with them, and this made him stand out.

Here is what you can do to practice empathy:

- ✓ Listen and do not interrupt.

- ✓ Put yourself into the other person's feelings.

✓ Recognize and appreciate your employee's effort. Remember that your employees are humans and not machines. Hence, take time to recognize their efforts and let them know how valuable they are to the company.

7. Give it your all.

Most of the time, you only have one shot to get it right. Therefore, you have to give all the best of you. You have to do your best in whatever you do. You have to pour your heart and soul into your work.

One of the best things about Gary Vaynerchuk is that he really gives everything that he got all the time. He always strives to provide the best to his clients and audience. He made sure that he is one step ahead of everyone else.

To succeed in life, you must pour everything in whatever you choose to do.

8. Do not over think.

Overthinking is dangerous because it slows you down. It also leads to diseases like anxiety and depression. It holds you back.

If you want to gain the right momentum and build a successful business, you must stop overthinking and start doing. You should stop thinking about what other people think about you because, the truth is, their opinions do not matter. Find a way to silence that noise in your mind.

9. Humor is the most attractive personality trait.

The path to business success is paved with problems and challenges. Therefore, you have to maintain a good sense of humor to keep your sanity and succeed in business.

Gary Vaynerchuk is driven. He is a go-getter. He goes after whatever he wants. He is confident in what he can do. Nevertheless, what is impressive about him is that he does not take himself too seriously. He has a great sense of humor that is quite infectious. He is not afraid to laugh at himself and his mistakes.

Here are some tips that you can use to improve your sense of humor:

- ✓ Watch something funny. This increases your sense of humor almost instantly.

- ✓ Be witty.

✓ Learn to laugh at yourself.

✓ Focus on the things that amuse you.

The sense of humor is a useful trait that you can use to succeed in business and life. So, laugh, smile, and do not be afraid to look silly every occasionally.

10. Be human.

Most entrepreneurs paint themselves as mythical and unreachable beings. However, Gary Vaynerchuk is different from these entrepreneurs. He is not afraid to show people who he is. He is not scared to show people his disappointments, excitement, failures, and challenges. He is not afraid to curse and announce to the world how much he appreciates his wife. He is brave enough to express his love for his parents. Gary Vaynerchuk is one of the most human multi-millionaires, and this is what made him stand out of the pack. He is not afraid to show his humanity to his fans.

11. Be grateful.

Gratitude is a magical tool that you can use to build a fulfilling life. It helps you appreciate your customers, employees, and investors.

Gratitude also increases your resilience. It helps you rise whenever you lose a client, or you are having a bad day at work. It helps you recover from losses and bad decisions.

Here are some tips that you can use in practicing gratitude in business:

✓ Keep a journal of all your challenges. Write down all the problems that you are currently facing in your business, like a demanding customer, or poor execution or your ideas. Then, be thankful for your problems. Writing your problems down with a grateful heart helps you put things in perspective. It helps you stop worrying about the problem and develop a solution. It takes your focus out of the problem, so you can start working on a solution.

✓ Write thank you letters to your customers. If your business is still new and you do not have many customers yet, it is a good idea to write "thank you" notes to your customers. This will make them feel valued. If you already have a strong social media following, take time to thank your followers for sticking with you.

✓ Let your employees know how much you appreciate them. People leave their jobs whenever they feel that they are underappreciated. So say, "thank you" often. This will motivate your employees to work harder and strive to be the best that they can be.

12. Take care of your health.

When Gary first appeared in the online world, he was chubby and might have been drinking a bit too much wine. When he left the wine world and ventured into social media marketing, and learned the value of taking care of his health. He learned that image is essential. Therefore, he hired a personal trainer named Mike Vacanti. Mike helped Gary get fit, and he taught him the value of proper nutrition.

Gary started eating well and, he began to take care of his body. Today, Gary is ripped and more attractive. He is at the peak of his health. This newfound attractiveness opened new doors for him. He was cast as one of the judges of the first Apple reality series, "The Planet of the Apps." He also got a lot of speaking engagements.

13. Give your children freedom.

When Gary was a young boy, he did not do well in school. He constantly got low grades. This made him feel inadequate, but Gary was lucky enough to have a very supportive mother. Gary's mother allowed him to blossom into the one thing that he was really good at – entrepreneurship.

As the philosopher Khalil Gibran once wrote – your children are not you. They have their own destinies and their own dreams. You can guide them, but do not decide what is best for them. Give them enough freedom to thrive in the things that they are actually good for them. Do not force them to study if they are not interested in school. Do not mold them into what your idea of success is.

For the most of his life, Gary worked in his family business, but he always knew that he is meant to do something else. He knew that he was destined for something higher than working in his father's wine shop.

Gary said that if you want your children to be the best that they can be, you have to give them freedom.

14. Care about other people.

Steve Jobs was successful. He built great things. His products are in almost every American home. However, in Gary Vaynerchuk's own words, he was "kind of a dick." He did not care about his employees. He did not care about other people. He drove people into extreme exhaustion.

There was a time when every entrepreneur is acting like a jerk because they wanted to be Steve Jobs. However, Steve Jobs is not the rule; he was the exemption. If you want to build a meaningful and long-lasting business, you have to care about other people. You have to show them compassion.

Gary Vaynerchuk believes that you cannot fake compassion. You have to show to your customers that you genuinely care about them. Do not be arrogant and say, "I'm richer than this guy so I will not give a damn about what he says or how he feels." Remember that you are nothing without your customers. Your business is nothing without your customers. Therefore, you have to go out of your way and show your customers that you care about them and that what they have to say is important to you.

Your employees are not tools; they are your partners. You are nothing without them. Do not be too proud and say that they are replaceable. Good employees are hard to find these days. So, be humble and recognize the value that your employees are giving you.

15. Always strive to do the right thing.

Many people think that entrepreneurs are shrewd and that they would do just about anything to make money. Well, it is true at some point. A few people got rich by stepping on other people and breaking laws. Nevertheless, if you want to sleep well at night, choose to do the right thing. Listen to what your heart is telling you, and if something does not feel right then do not do it. Your reputation, integrity, and conscience are more important than your success in business. You must seek to achieve business success in the right way.

16. There are more important things than business and money.

Being rich is good. In fact, being rich is much better than being poor. Gary said that it was good that he was able to provide for his wife, Lizzie, and their kids. He is happy that his kids will not go through all the hardships that he went through as a child. However, he is much more proud of the emotional support that he provides to his kids than all the vacations and cool stuff.

17. You should be a practitioner.

There are a lot of gurus and experts online, but the problem with them is that they are all talk and no action. If you want to build a solid reputation as an entrepreneur, you have to be a practitioner.

Gary believes that you do not learn stuff by reading alone, you learn by doing. Although Gary wrote several self-help books, he does not read a lot of them himself. The things that he teaches in his writings he learned firsthand by doing them.

18. Listen to yourself.

Listening to others helps you put things in perspective. It enables you learn new things. It helps you get feedback. However, to make right life decisions, you must listen to yourself first.

19. Do not bring your work troubles home.

Gary Vaynerchuk is a workaholic. He works at least 12 hours a day, but he is wise enough to separate his work life from his home life. He does not take his work troubles home. He leaves his work stress at his office and makes sure that he is on his best behavior when facing his wife and kids.

Gary said that he separated his work and home life by using one crucial tool – gratitude. He is so grateful that he got to work hard, so he thinks that it is unfair to his wife, Lizzie, and their kids if he allows his work problems affect his mood at home.

20. Take responsibility for your life. Take the blame

One of the best things about Gary Vaynerchuk is that he continually says something that many people would not say, "It's my fault." It takes a lot of security, confidence, and courage to say these words.

You see, most of us spend our days blaming other people for the things that happened in our lives. We blame the government, our parents, or our spouses for all the mistakes that we have made.

However, you cannot blame other people forever. At some point, you have to take responsibility for everything that happened in your life. Gary said that if you want to be a successful businessperson, you have to be willing to take the heat. Saying "It's my fault" does not make you a lesser person. In fact, it allows you to win other people's respect. It makes you a strong and confident leader. It makes you stand out.

So, instead of wasting time blaming others, just admit that it is your fault, learn from the mistake, and move on. That is the only way that you will learn.

21. Self-awareness sells.

Self-awareness is powerful because it allows you to live courageously. It encourages authenticity. This makes you intensely attractive and magnetic. If you want to attract all the right people and opportunities in your life be aware of who you are. Know your strengths, your weakness, and your dreams. Self-awareness is a powerful tool that helps you draw other people into your world and get them to buy whatever you are selling – products, services, and even ideas.

22. How you make money is just as important as how much money you actually make.

Many online entrepreneurs engage in shady practices just to earn money. Some of these 'entrepreneurs' rent planes and luxury cars to project an image of fake success.

Gary believes in the power of doing honest business transactions. You must observe truth in selling and deliver what you promised to the customer. You must also keep integrity in accounting and management practices.

23. Giving up is not an option.

If you want to create something unusual, you have to keep going even when you encounter problems day in and day out.

24. Surround yourself with winners.

Misery is contagious. Therefore, to push yourself forward, you have to surround yourself with winners, or people who are already successful. You have to associate yourself with A-plus generals.

When Gary ran the wine shop, he was virtually unknown. Hence, he invested in big-name companies like Twitter and Facebook to get access to the big players in the social media industry.

25. Do not fake it 'till you make it.

Gary Vaynerchuk does not believe in the old entrepreneurship slogan "fake it 'till you make it". He thinks that it is bad advice because it is stressful, and it ruins you financially. So, instead of following the "fake it until you make it" business advice, believe in yourself one hundred percent. Instead of saying "I am already successful," say, "I believe that I can be successful." Genuine self-confidence is far more powerful than faking it.

Gary Vaynerchuk is not only succeeding in business, but he has also succeeded in life, and he is just getting started.

Final Thoughts

Gary Vaynerchuk is loud, and he looks like the generic egomaniac entrepreneur, but the truth is that he is just a passionate soul who dreams of making it in the big evil world of business. He is indeed the poster boy of the American Dream. He came from a poor immigrant family that did not speak English. He was fortunate to have a hardworking father who practically handed him the family wine business. Nevertheless, his father did not hand the wine shop to Gary on a silver platter; he has to work hard for it.

Gary knew that he is a gifted entrepreneur. He knew that selling was his most significant passion. He also knew that marketing is his biggest skill. Therefore, he used all that passion, drive, and skills to build a name for himself. He had a great father who taught him the value of entrepreneurship, but it was his own efforts that put him on the business map. Because of that, he is a real inspiration.

Here is a list of the main points and the lessons of this book:

- ✓ It is okay if you are not born rich. You can rise from your current situation and build something for yourself, no matter who you are and where you are from.

✓ School is good because it gives you security, but they are not designed for entrepreneurs, they are intended for employees. If you want to be a prominent entrepreneur like Gary Vaynerchuk, you must learn by doing.

✓ Use the power of social media to tell your story. Many people think that social networking sites are nothing but distractions and a waste of time. Moreover, at some point, this is true but, you can use the power of social media to create a personal brand. You can use it to tell your story.

✓ Take care of your customers. You will not have a business if not for your customers. Therefore, you have to put your customers first. You have to listen to them and engage them. Reply to their comments and messages.

✓ Be confident. What is fascinating about Gary Vee is his confidence. He really believes in himself. He believes that he is the best in the business and that he can do it. You cannot help but also believe in him.

Gary Vee is the classic example of someone who is really crushing it. Someone who successfully climbed the ladder of business success.

✓ Always give value to your customers. Produce high-quality content and high-quality products.

✓ Stick to your DNA and always be true to who you are.

✓ You have to get yourself noticed. During his early days, many netizens called Gary a "famewhore" because he was just everywhere. However, you cannot really make a name for yourself if you do not put yourself out there. So, do not hold back. Self-promotion is good for you, especially if you are trying to be a multi-million entrepreneur.

✓ Work with a formidable team. Gary appears as if he did it all. Nevertheless, he would not get to where he is right now if not for his incredible team.

✓ Do not put all your eggs in one basket. Gary Vaynerchuk understands that you cannot build maximum wealth if you just focus on the business that you created. You have to invest in other people's businesses, too. Gary was wise enough to invest in profitable tech companies such as Twitter, Facebook, Tumblr and Birchbox.

✓ Put your family first. Always remember that even if you own half of New York City, your family will still be your most precious possession.

✓ I hope that Gary's story has motivated you to give your best in everything that you do, and this book was able to inspire you to follow your passion and go beyond your failures. You are born poor, so what? You are not good at school, so what? You are not your circumstances. You are not your grade. You are what you do. So, stop moping around and get work as hard as Gary Vaynerchuk did.

Thank you for downloading this book, and I hope that you enjoy it.

Claim Your Free Bonuses

Here's a reminder to claim your free bonuses! Click here now or visit http://goodread.site/premium-bonus-gary-vee/ to claim your free bonuses now!

Thank you! We really hope that you've enjoyed reading this book! Could you help us? Leaving an honest review on our book will greatly help us turn those feedbacks into improvements in the long term!

P.S. If you have 30 seconds to spare, click here or visit

https://www.amazon.com/review/create-review

to leave us an honest review now. Thank you so much

Made in the USA
Lexington, KY
07 April 2018